P9-CMQ-516

Junior High School

airsville, Pennsylvania

Nancy Henderson

LEFT: The Santa Eulalia River, principal tributary of the Rimac.

ABOVE: Harvesting wheat in the Mantaro Valley, two miles high.

Nancy Henderson

Engine No. 224 thunders out of a tunnel and over the Rimac River.

<small>THE</small> Rimac

River of Peru

ALEXANDER L. CROSBY

Map by Fred Kliem

GARRARD PUBLISHING COMPANY
CHAMPAIGN, ILLINOIS

THIS BOOK WAS EDITED AND DESIGNED
UNDER THE SUPERVISION OF NANCY LARRICK, ED.D.

For reading the manuscript of this book and checking
its accuracy, the author and editor are indebted to
Peter A. Lara, Latin-American specialist of the Peace
Corps. Separate chapters were read and criticized by
René Moosman of Lima Light and Power Company
and by Archibald Leishman of the Central Railway
of Peru. Miss Vera Neuwald of Universal Travels,
Lima, then of Lima Light and Power Company, arranged the tour of the Transandean tunnel project.
  Dr. Mario Hangartner introduced us to Lima and its
environs. The people of Peru gave warm cooperation.

Copyright © 1966 by Alexander L. Crosby

All rights reserved. Manufactured in the U.S.A.

Library of Congress Catalog Card Number: 67-10021

Nancy Henderson

Nevado Rajuntay Mountain, 18,635 feet, is typical of the Andes.

Contents

Life for the Desert 5

The Indian Terraces 10

The Spanish Ruffian 18

Wonderful Fertilizer 27

The Highest Railroad in the World 35

Smoke on the Mountains 48

Gifts from Peru 58

Tunnel Through the Andes 66

Lima Today 77

The Squatters 83

End of the River 90

Index 95

PACIFIC OCEAN

HUACHO

ANCÓN

CALLAO

LIMA

PACHACAMAC

CHOSICA

RIO

SANTA EULALIA

RIMAC

RIO EULALIA

MATUCANA

SAN BARTOLOME

HUINCO

TRANSANDEAN TUNNEL

MOROCOCHA

CERRO DE PASCO

LAGO PUNRÚN

LAGUNA JUNIN

JUNIN

LA OROYA

RIO MANTARO

HUANCA

HUANCAVELICA

CAÑETE

CHINCHA ALTA

PISCO

STATUTE MILES

0   25   50   75

Life for the Desert

Not many years after Columbus, one of the earliest Spanish navigators was, asked how the coast of Peru could be recognized. "When you see no more trees, it will be Peru," the explorer said.

The long coast of Peru is indeed a desert. It runs for more than 1,400 miles, from Ecuador into Chile. The waves of the Pacific Ocean tumble upon a beach that is as bare as the land close behind it.

A few miles from the ocean, the foothills of the Andes begin. Sailors have long viewed these mountains with awe. They rise to heights of three and four miles, forming a jagged ridge. Airplane passengers get an even more spectacular view of snow-capped ranges.

Twisting down from the peaks are deep ravines and gorges. Water from rain and melting snow has carved them over millions of years. On the eastern slope these streams become tributaries of the Amazon and flow through the jungle into the Atlantic Ocean.

On the western slope the mountain streams empty into the Pacific. About 60 rivers knife through the strip of desert to reach the ocean. The bottomland in their narrow valleys is green, because it has long been irrigated with river water. The hillsides are dry and brown. Every little breeze stirs a cloud of dust.

The Rimac is Peru's most important river. It is hardly 80 miles long. It isn't wide—any healthy child could throw a stone across it. But it has done more than any other river to shape the nation. On the river's ancient flood plain, eight miles from the ocean, stands the great city of Lima. At the river's mouth is Callao, the country's main seaport. One-fourth of Peru's population is in the Lima-Callao area. These people depend on the Rimac for water and for electric power. The river

Nancy Henderson

Each llama is carrying a bag of grain along the road by the Rimac.

also provides a route for one of Peru's two railroads across the Andes.

Although the Rimac is little more than a creek during the dry season, it becomes a raging torrent when the snows melt in the mountains. The flood plain is solidly packed with stones that have been rounded and polished by the river. Each stone was once a tiny fragment of the Andes.

The word "Rimac" is from the ancient Quechua

7

Nancy Henderson

Rimac water is hauled on a bicycle wheel cart and by burro back.

language of Peru. It means "the speaker." "Lima" is a corrupted form of Rimac and was once written as Limac.

Centuries ago the first European visitors wondered why it rarely rained along the coast of Peru. There are two reasons. First, the soaring peaks of the Andes block the moist trade winds from the east. The trade winds bring rain to the jungle on the eastern slope of the Andes. Water is plentiful there.

But on the west, the cool Humboldt current

8

Nancy Henderson

The water gushing from the culvert is the start of the Rimac River.

prevents rain from falling along the coast. On other seacoasts, warm, moist air from the ocean condenses when it meets cool air high in the sky. Not in Peru. The ocean air is already cooled before it moves inland. It is cooled by the Humboldt current, which flows north from the region of the South Pole. There is no rainfall when this cool air meets more cool air above the land. There is only a fine drizzle, little more than fog. It is called the *garua*, and the people of Lima complain about it from April to November.

9

The Indian Terraces

Long before the Spaniards came to the New World, terraced gardens were built along the steep sides of the Rimac Valley. Many are still standing and still being used. They are the work of the Indians, who were good engineers and superb farmers.

In a country where tillable land is scarce, every square foot of good soil is valuable. It means another meal. So, all over Peru, the Indians turned the mountainsides into gardens. They dug long aqueducts to bring river water for irrigation.

Until the Spaniards conquered Peru in 1532, all of the people were Indians. They made up the main part of the great Inca empire, ruled from

Nancy Henderson

Peru's mountains were terraced for gardens hundreds of years ago.

Cuzco in the central highlands. Today the pure-blooded Indians are only about 40 percent of the population. Most of the people are whites or mestizos (of mixed Indian and white blood).

The Rimac flows through mountain country where the Indians live. But their life is quite different today. Only a few have their own small farms. Many more are employed on the big estates, called haciendas, or in the mines. Some

11

Nancy Henderson

A school lunch program for three lambs in the lower Rimac Valley.

have jobs in the small towns along the river: Chaclacayo, Chosica, Surco, Matucana and San Mateo. Others work for the railroad. Some drive the dusty buses that whine up and down the unpaved highway, skirting precipices as if they were no more than roadside ditches.

Yet the past has not been entirely buried. There are still llamas to be seen in the high country. Indian women still spin wool with a short stick

12

that has a spool at the end. They move it up and down, hardly looking at their quick fingers. And when the highway climbs from the desert into the zone of light rainfall, the roadside is brightened with a dozen kinds of wildflowers. They are the same plants that once bloomed along the Incas' trails.

The Incas spoke a language called Quechua, and it is still spoken in the highlands. But the Incas had no written language. They kept records of their history with curiously knotted strings, called *quipus*. Men were trained to remember what each knot meant. When there were no more rememberers, there was no more recorded history.

Yet archeologists and historians have discovered a great deal about the ancient civilizations of Peru. They have read books written by the early Spaniards. They have examined the ruins of buildings. They have studied pictures on pottery and textiles, and relics from tombs. They have used aerial photography to find the sites of lost cities. And the carbon-14 method has enabled them to date many of their findings. This is a system for

American Museum of Natural History
This ancient Peruvian jar has a whistle in the belly of the cat.

measuring radioactivity in wood, mummies and other things that once lived. Using a Geiger counter, a scientist can quickly estimate age.

Peru had many ancient civilizations before the rise of the Incas. The Paracas culture along the coast, south of Lima, dates from 400 B.C. These people wove the finest textiles that have ever been found. Still older was the Chavin culture, which began in 1200 B.C. Its center was in the Andes,

14

north of the Rimac. Its symbol was the fierce Cat God.

Some of these cultures lasted for only a few hundred years, others much longer. Then, in the valley of Cuzco, a powerful tribe took root in about A.D. 1000. These people were the Incas.

The Incas said they had been chosen by the Sun God to improve the life of other Indians. They spent almost 500 years carrying out their program. First they had to conquer those who needed improvement. Then they organized the defeated tribes.

Families were grouped into communes, where everyone shared land, animals and the harvest. The commune elected its leader, who was assisted by a council of old men. There was a straw boss for each 10 workers, a foreman for each 10 straw bosses and a supervisor for each 10 foremen. A tribe of 10,000 workers had a chief, who was under a provincial governor. The governor took his orders from the ruler of one of the four quarters of the Inca empire. The four rulers reported directly to the emperor.

Most of the men worked in the fields and gardens. They took seeds and roots from wild plants that could be eaten. Over hundreds of years they improved these wildlings. Victor W. von Hagen, the archeologist, has pointed out that more than half of the world's foods were developed by the farmers of the Andes. Among them are corn, potatoes, sweet potatoes, squashes, beans, manioc, tomatoes, peppers, peanuts, cashews, avocados, strawberries, mulberries, pineapples and papayas.

The Incas grew at least 20 kinds of corn, including popcorn. And they had a method for turning potatoes into a flour that could be stored in granaries for years.

When the emperors needed soldiers, the farmers were summoned. The farmers also built the famous roads that linked the provinces of the empire. One Inca highway, 24 feet wide, ran 2,500 miles along the coast, from Tumbes, Peru, to Santiago, Chile. Thirsty couriers refreshed themselves where the road crossed the Rimac.

The Incas' use of stone was almost unbelievable. Huge rocks weighing many tons were moved from

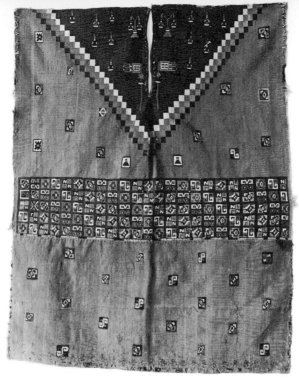

American Museum of Natural History
The Incas wove this poncho centuries ago.

quarries to the site of a temple or fortress. They were shaped with primitive tools and fitted together without mortar. The joints were so tight a knife blade could not be forced into them.

Crime and falsehood were almost unheard of. One of the Spanish conquerors wrote that "an Indian with 100,000 pieces of gold and silver in his house left it open, only placing a little stick across the door, as the sign that the master was out, and nobody went in." Except, of course, the highly civilized Spaniards.

The Spanish Ruffian

In 1529 an illiterate ruffian named Francisco Pizarro got a magnificent gift from King Charles of Spain. He was authorized to help himself to a large portion of Peru, provided he would share his loot with the king. Three years later, with less than 200 men, Pizarro faced the Inca emperor, Atahualpa. The Spaniards had reached Cajamarca, in the northern part of Peru, after terrible hardships.

The Inca had several thousand warriors on foot. Pizarro was counting on four things: horses, guns, armor and treachery. He attacked in the midst of a peaceful meeting, and the Indians were slaughtered by the hundreds. Not one Spaniard died.

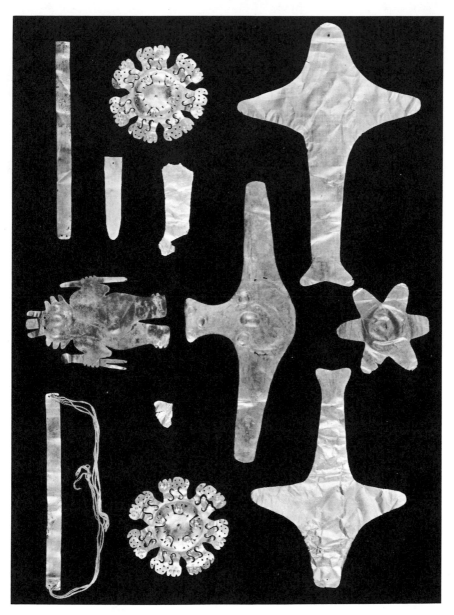

American Museum of Natural History

What the Spaniards wanted: gold. All this was on a mummy's head.

Nancy Henderson   *Lehigh University Library*

In years past the Rimac gorge was crossed as shown in the drawing.

Atahualpa was captured. He offered to buy his freedom. For a ransom, he promised to fill a large room in his palace with gold, and then twice with silver. Pizarro accepted greedily. Indian runners were dispatched to Cuzco, 750 miles south, with the emperor's orders. Each man ran four or five miles to a station where fresh runners were waiting. A message could be carried 150 miles in one day, even in the high mountains. The pony express of 1860 covered only 250 miles with fast horses.

Gold vases, gold plate, gold ornaments and tons of silver soon poured into Cajamarca. Two thousand Indians carried the ransom. Atahualpa had kept his pledge. But instead of being turned loose, he was killed by Pizarro.

Now master of the Inca empire, Pizarro decided to build a capital city on the coast. In 1535 he went to the Rimac River and laid out the city of Lima. He did not live to see Lima in its glory. Spanish enemies invaded his house in 1541 and killed him.

Lima grew and prospered from the wealth of the country. Two centuries after its founding, the ruling families adorned themselves, their houses and their churches with silver and gold, pearls and diamonds, velvet and lace. The cathedral and the five largest churches were treasure houses. Altars were covered with heavy silver, from the floor up. The main aisles had rows of silver candlesticks that were taller than most Indians. At the Church of Our Lady of Rosario, the monstrance for sacred relics was a gorgeous vessel. It sparkled with 1,304 diamonds, 1,029 emeralds, 522 rubies, 121 pearls, 45 amethysts and 2 topazes.

Most of Lima's wealth came from trade. Cargoes from Spain and from ports in New Spain filled the warehouses of Callao. Caravans of pack mules came from Paita, a seaport 600 miles north. Their trail through the coastal desert was marked by the whitened bones of animals that had died along the way. To avoid the scorching sun and blistering sand, the caravans traveled by night.

Lima was the great distribution center for all of Peru. Through its gates went iron, copper, tin, naphtha, tar, lumber, textiles, indigo, tea, wine, raisins, olives, wheat, tobacco, porcelain, pearls, perfume and a thousand other items. Pack trains carried the merchandise over tortuous trails to the cities of the mountains. Foaming rivers were crossed on suspension bridges made from twisted vines or braided skins. On the return trip, the animals carried bars of silver and the products of the mountains.

Although Lima had only 15,000 whites in 1740,

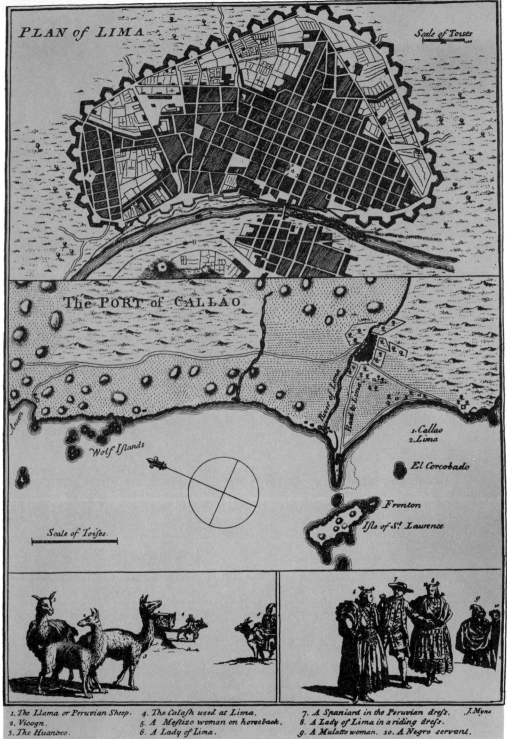

PLAN of LIMA

Scale of Toises

The PORT of CALLAO

Anson

Wolf Islands

River of Lima

Road to Lima

1. Callao
2. Lima

El Corcobado

Scale of Toises.

Fronton

Isle of St. Lawrence

1. The Llama or Peruvian Sheep.
2. Vicogn.
3. The Huanoco.

4. The Calash used at Lima.
5. A Mestizo woman on horseback.
6. A Lady of Lima.

7. A Spaniard in the Peruvian dress.
8. A Lady of Lima in a riding dress.
9. A Mulatto woman. 10. A Negro servant.

J. Myns

Lehigh University Library

Lima was once a walled city, and the Rimac was the "River of Lima."

it boasted some 45 counts and marquises, plus a number of knights in military orders. The Spanish ladies were dark-haired beauties, at least in their youth. Husbands and fathers spent vast sums for their upkeep. A lady could not be happy with a dress made from the finest material. The finest material had to be covered with the finest lace, and the finest lace came only from Flanders.

The hair of a stylish lady was made into six long braids. These were tied up at the back of the head with a gold bodkin, decorated with diamonds at each end. From the bodkin the locks fell to the shoulder. Diamond ornaments were worn over the forehead, and the hair in front was formed into curls that hung down to the ears. The well-dressed woman also wore diamond earrings, diamond bracelets, diamond rings, diamond neck-laces and diamond shoe buckles. Sometimes she displayed at her waist a large jewel, encircled with diamonds. Her garters were embroidered with gold or silver, sometimes set with pearls.

The streets of Lima were filled with the vehicles of the upper-class families. The rich rode in four-

Lehigh University Library

Balsa rafts were made by the Indians for use in the Pacific Ocean.

wheeled coaches and the not-so-rich had two-wheeled chaises with facing seats for two or four persons. There were about 5,000 of these two-wheelers, drawn by mules.

Peru was governed by a viceroy, appointed by the king of Spain. The viceroy's power was tremendous, and his decisions were rarely appealed. All kinds of people came to his palace daily, seeking help or favors. The Indians and Negroes

25

Blairsville Junior High School
Blairsville, Pennsylvania

were received in one chamber. A second chamber was reserved for Spaniards, and a third chamber was used by ladies who wished to speak privately.

When a new viceroy was appointed, he was welcomed to Lima like a king. City officials, the military and church organizations joined in a general celebration. Costly gifts were showered on the new ruler. The givers all hoped, of course, that their generosity would be remembered.

As the eighteenth century closed, the gilded glory of Spain was losing its luster. The Indians had been cruelly abused for 250 years. For example, one law forbade them to cut their hair. Spanish overseers found long hair useful when they dragged Indian workers to their tasks.

In 1781 the Indians revolted, but the Spaniards put a bloody end to the rebellion. Finally, in 1821, Peru won the aid of the Argentine liberator, José de San Martín. The Peruvians declared their independence, and Spain gave up.

Rómulo Jordán, Instituto del Mar del Peru
Each guanay produces about 35 pounds of valuable fertilizer a year.

Wonderful Fertilizer

Sometimes huge red patches appear in the ocean off the coast of Peru. The patches are alive. They are formed by millions of tiny crustaceans, which are gobbled up by vast numbers of fish and birds.

The cool Humboldt current that flows along the Peruvian coast has the right temperature for plankton and many kinds of creatures. Anchovies

27

and other small fishes thrive in countless numbers. This great feeding ground has supported hungry sea birds for ages. Among the most important birds are (1) the *guanay*, a white-breasted cormorant; (2) the *piquero*, a booby or gannet; and (3) the *alcatraz*, a pelican.

When vast flocks of these birds go fishing, the spectacle is almost beyond description. Dr. Frank M. Chapman of the American Museum of Natural History told what he saw from a ship in 1918:

> The Cormorants fished from the surface, where they were evidently surrounded by a sea of the small fry, which, with much plunging and diving, they gobbled voraciously, until, their storage capacity reached, they rested in great black rafts on the water, waiting for the processes of digestion to give both excuse and space for further gorging.
>
> The Boobies fished from the air, plunging headlong and with great force from an average height of fifty feet into the water

almost directly. Like a great flying spearhead they strike the water and disappear in the jet of foam which spurts upward as they hit the surface. It is a more thrilling, reckless performance than even the plunge of the Fish Hawk. But the most amazing phenomenon in all this amazing scene was the action of flocks of Boobies of five hundred to a thousand birds, which, in more or less compact formation, were hurrying to join one of the Booby squalls which darkened the air over the fishing grounds. If, unexpectedly, they chanced to fly over a school of fish, instantly every Booby in the flock plunged downward and in a twinkling the air, which had been filled with rapidly flying birds, was left without a feather! This spectacle, the most surprising evolution I have ever seen in bird life, was witnessed repeatedly during the day.

No wonder this booby is known as the piquero (pee-KAIR-o), which is Spanish for "lancer."

American Museum of Natural History

Guanayes nest close together on an island off the coast of Peru.

After a hard day's eating, the birds return to their roosting places on small, rocky islands off the shore. As in Lima, there is no rainfall on these islands. Over thousands of years the treeless surfaces have worn a white crown from the droppings of the birds.

This manure, called *guano* (GWAH-no), is rich in nitrogen. It makes wonderful fertilizer—about 30 times better than barnyard manure. The ancient Incas knew the value of guano. They carried it from the islands and up the river valleys, where the mountain slopes were terraced for gardens. Thanks to the sea birds, the Incas raised good crops.

American Museum of Natural History
Thousands of guanayes darken the beach on North Chincha Island.

The Indians took only a tiny part of the rich deposits. They did not disturb the nesting birds. And so the layers of guano kept building up, often to a height of 100 feet or more above the rocks. Most of the deposits came from the guanay, or white-breasted cormorant. Dr. Robert Cushman

31

Nancy Henderson

Guano makes cotton grow, but only the rich own tractors in Peru.

Murphy has called this cormorant "the most valuable bird in the world."

In 1843 Peru began selling guano in foreign markets. Greedy officials saw a chance to make money for themselves as well as for the government. Soon hundreds of ships came to the islands. Chinese coolies were imported as slaves to dig the guano. Overseers stood over them with whips, forcing them to dig five tons a day, every day in the year. Nearly every week one of the coolies committed suicide by jumping from a cliff. Most had given up hope of ever getting back to China.

32

The birds fared no better than the Chinese. Thousands of nests were destroyed, and many birds were killed or frightened away. But nobody worried about the future while guano was bringing twenty or thirty million dollars into Peru each year. When the government borrowed money, the guano deposits served as security. Foreign investors knew that guano was as good as gold.

It was, but by 1900 the ancient supply was giving out. The end of the guano industry was near. Then, as if by a miracle, ruin was prevented. In 1909 the government acted to protect the birds and to regulate the digging of guano. Every island was declared a bird sanctuary and trespassers were barred. Passing ships were forbidden to blow their whistles. An official agency, The Guano Company, was set up to run the business. After guano had been dug from an island, the birds were to be left alone for two or three years. Then the fresh supply could be harvested.

The new system has worked. The bird flocks have increased. The farmers of Peru now have a regular supply of guano.

It is estimated that a single bird eats 172 pounds of fish each year. The bird leaves 35 pounds of guano on one of the islands. This will sell for $1.50 to $2. Since there are more than 20 million birds, the profits are sizable.

A new threat to the birds has arisen since World War II. Peru has at last developed a fishing industry. The country has become the world's largest exporter of fishmeal, used for animal food and for fertilizer. There are some 40 fishmeal plants around Callao and Lima, and the smell is awful.

Fishmeal is made from the same little anchovies that the cormorants, the boobies and the pelicans eat. For every two fishes eaten by the birds, a third fish goes into the cooker at one of the factories. Will there be enough anchovies to keep the birds well fed? Scientists of The Guano Company are concerned. They are studying the life history of the anchovy. They want to find out why the schools get larger in some years, smaller in others. They want to make sure that the most valuable bird in the world does not starve to death.

C. Crofton Atkins

A Central Railway freight on the Meiggs siding, three miles high.

The Highest Railroad
in the World

The towns and cities of the Andes grew up in loneliness. There were no roads from one to another because there were no wagons or carts. The wheel was not known to the Incas. People traveled on foot along rough trails. Freight was carried on their backs, or by llamas.

The llama, a small relative of the camel, is still

35

a valued animal in the high mountains. It requires little food and water. It provides both wool and meat. But it has one bad habit: spitting. Anyone who tries to make a weary llama keep moving is apt to get his face sprayed with smelly saliva.

Like the mountain people, the llama can work where the air is thin. At an elevation of three miles oxygen becomes scarce. People not used to this height suffer from *soroche*, or mountain sickness. They feel dizzy, get headaches and sometimes vomit.

There was not much oxygen along the old foot trail up the Rimac Valley and across the Andes to La Oroya. The trail skirted precipices above the churning river. It climbed bare rock with steps chiseled into the stone. It zigzagged higher and higher, opening vistas of naked mountains capped with snow.

Building a railway up the Rimac Valley looked impossible. The valley was too steep for trains. The rocky walls of the mountains had no ledges where tracks could be laid. Many engineers said the idea was hopeless.

Nancy Henderson

Llamas carried much of the freight before the railway was opened.

Nancy Henderson

Heading up the Rimac, a passenger train approaches a switchback.

But Peru was being swept by railroad fever in the 1860s. Political leaders declared that railroads would bring prosperity to the whole country. And there was one man in Peru who swore that he

Nancy Henderson

The train has switched to the higher track and is now backing up.

could lay track anywhere that a llama could go.

This man was Henry Meiggs, a native of New York, who had made and lost a fortune in the California gold rush. He had secretly sailed from

39

San Francisco in 1854 after forging more than $350,000 in city warrants. He had landed in Chile and proved his skill as a railroad builder. By 1869 he was building Peru's first major railroad, from Mollendo on the coast to Arequipa in the Andes.

Before the Arequipa line was finished, Meiggs got a government contract to build a railroad through the Rimac Valley from Callao to La Oroya. Work began in January 1870.

The obstacles were tremendous. There were places where surveyors had to be lowered on ropes to mark the route along cliffs. Days were spent in blasting footholds and building temporary roads for mules.

There was no room in the narrow valley for the railroad to climb gradually with long, sweeping curves. But the track had to rise with the sharply rising river. The solution was to build switchbacks, or zigzags. The track would come to a dead end, usually near the river bottom. Then another track would fork upward and backward. The train would back up this fork until it came to another switchback, much higher up. Then it would go forward again.

The line from Callao to La Oroya is only 138 miles long. But it has 19 switchbacks, 59 bridges and 66 tunnels. At one point the train shoots out of a tunnel and roars across a high bridge over the Rimac—then disappears in another tunnel.

The highest point on the line is 15,681 feet. This is at Galera, where the track runs through Mount Meiggs. There is no other standard gauge railroad, anywhere in the world, as high as that. The steepest grade is 4.42%, which means the railroad climbs 4.42 feet in a distance of 100 feet. The limit for most railroads in the United States is 2%.

Almost everything needed for the building of the railroad had to be imported. Iron and coal came from Great Britain. Bridges, the first locomotives and most of the timber and ties came from the United States. Food for workers and the mules came from California and Chile. More than 500 mules were used to haul supplies forward, where track had not been laid.

Meiggs was prepared to conquer the Andes, but his troubles were worse than the mountains. Thousands of workmen were stricken by the

mysterious Oroya fever. (Years later it was traced to the bite of an insect.) Thousands died—nobody knows how many. Meiggs had imported many of his workers from Chile, and the frightened Chileans wanted to go home. Many left the construction site and headed for Lima.

In California there were thousands of Chinese who had helped to build the first transcontinental railroad. In China millions more were ready to sail for America. Meiggs began to bring in Chinese workers, and the rails pushed forward. The Chinese were superior to the tough Chileans in two ways: they didn't drink and they didn't fight.

But neither the Chinese nor the Chileans could work well when the railroad reached high altitudes of the Rimac Valley. They were not used to the scanty supply of oxygen. Meiggs turned then to the native Indians, the *serranos*, who could work all day long. Each man got two pounds of food a day: one pound of corn, and one pound of stew made from meat, potatoes, rice, beans and flour. A day's pay was about $1. The rate went up and

Highest point on the railroad: The tunnel under Mt. Meiggs, photographed through a train window.

Nancy Henderson

down, depending on how hard or easy it was to find men.

Meiggs, the Yankee who could build anything, failed to finish the railroad. He laid track 87 miles to Chicla and was 20 miles short of the summit when work stopped in 1875. Both Meiggs and Peru had run out of money. The government had borrowed money for the railroad by pledging the nation's income from guano sales. It had tried to float another big loan in 1872, but foreign investors bought very few bonds. The country was bankrupt.

Meiggs died in 1877 and was given a spectacular funeral.

Two years later Peru was at war with Chile. Lima was occupied by the enemy, and peace was not restored until 1883. Peru was in worse shape than ever. There was no money to complete the railroad. But in 1890 a British company took over the road, and three years later the tracks reached La Oroya. The little town on the eastern slope of the Andes had waited 23 years for the sight of a steam locomotive.

In the rugged mountains 84 miles northwest of

Nancy Henderson

Waiting for a truck, just across the Rimac from the Central Railway.

La Oroya were the Cerro de Pasco mines. Silver, gold and copper had been mined there for centuries. But it was hard and costly to haul ore on the backs of mules and llamas. Cerro de Pasco was almost a dead mining town.

A group of United States capitalists got an idea. Why not build a railroad from La Oroya to the mines? Then modern machinery could be brought to Cerro de Pasco, and the ore could be hauled

45

Nancy Henderson

Eucalyptus trees and eucalyptus logs in the rail yard at Huancayo.

out cheaply. J. Pierpont Morgan, Henry Clay Frick and a few other capitalists organized the Cerro de Pasco Copper Corporation. They built the railroad in 1904, and in 1922 they opened a great smelter at La Oroya. Profits from the mines have soared to countless millions, thanks to the low wage scale. Yet the daily wage of about $1.50 in the mines is far above the pittance paid to Peruvian farm workers.

More railroad building followed the mining boom. Seventy-seven miles southeast of La Oroya was the city of Huancayo (Wahn-KAI-o) on the Mantaro River. It was the center of a broad farming region with many smaller towns. But Huancayo was cut off from Lima and the coast. It did not have even a good highway route, much less a railroad. So in 1908 the Central Railway of Peru, as the Meiggs line was named, extended its track from La Oroya to Huancayo. Construction along the Mantaro River was fairly easy, because the river made a gradual descent on its long journey to the Amazon.

The Mantaro Valley has many groves of eucalyptus trees. Seeds were brought from Australia nearly 100 years ago. Since there is no native timber in the Andes, the eucalyptus has proved valuable. The Central Railway hauls thousands of logs for use as railroad ties and pit props in the mines.

Smoke
on the Mountains

The express train from Lima to Huancayo, 206 miles across the Andes, leaves Desamparados station at 7 o'clock each morning. *Desamparados* means "the afflicted ones." The station was named after a convent which once stood there and gave shelter to poor and homeless people.

The four of us—Nancy Henderson and her son, my wife and I—were lucky. We had tickets on that July morning in 1964 for one of the last expresses to be hauled by a steam locomotive. The Central Railway of Peru was changing to diesel engines.

Our locomotive was No. 224, a perky little

Nancy Henderson

Engine No. 224 crosses the Rimac as it begins to climb the Andes.

Consolidation type with a pony truck and four driving wheels. There were four passenger coaches and a buffet car with tables. The coaches were modern, built in England of light-weight steel to avoid extra weight on the steep grades. We had reserved seats in the buffet, which was never quite full.

Few working people in Peru own cars; almost

everybody travels by bus or railroad. Our Peruvian fellow passengers were a wonderful lot, more interesting and more friendly than the handful of tourists. Some carried dilapidated suitcases, held together with cords. Others had bundles and paper bags.

The train left the neatly swept station on time and headed up the Rimac Valley. We passed fields of cotton and corn. Onions, lettuce and sweet potatoes were growing on truck farms. It was hard to remember that July was the middle of Peru's winter.

Most farms were enclosed with low walls made from mud and the rounded stones of the river bottom. Around some houses there were high brick walls with broken glass along the top to discourage prowlers.

At Chosica, 25 miles from Lima and half a mile above sea level, we found something beautiful: sunshine. It was a welcome change from the gray clouds that cover Lima in this season. While the locomotive took on water, we stood on the platform near a group of laughing schoolboys. One

Nancy Henderson

The locomotive is pushed around on the turntable at San Bartolome.

of them, proud of his English, asked, "What is your name?" Without waiting for an answer he continued, "My name is Wilfred."

East of Chosica, the valley narrowed as the mountains rose. What mountains! They were

Nancy Henderson

Two first-class passengers at lunch in the railway's buffet car.

naked, adorned with nothing more than a few
clumps of cactus and a vast number of boulders.
Yet there was plenty of greenery in the valley,
irrigated by water from the Rimac. We saw
banana palms, pepper trees, oleanders and orchards
of apples and pears. One orchard had a crude

52

Nancy Henderson

Many passengers bought steaming ears of corn at a station stop.

tower made from poles, with a roof of small branches. It was a lookout, to guard against fruit thieves.

At San Bartolomé we made another stop. The locomotive was cut off and run onto a turntable. This was the first switchback. Because the next switchback was some 20 miles ahead, the locomotive was turned around to head the train.

Most of the other switchbacks were closer together, and the train simply backed uphill. The trainmen worked fast. The train would slow down and quickly come to a stop. There would be a pause of a few moments while the switch was thrown. Then, barely slowing to pick up the brakeman, No. 224 would make the valley echo with the blasts from its stack.

The track curved constantly as we climbed higher and higher. The curves were so sharp that we could see the engine and the first two or three cars going around the bend.

Toward noon the train stopped at a station where hot food was ready. Women on the platform ran to the doors and windows of the coaches, holding paper plates filled with meat and corn on the cob. Crusts and other leavings were snatched up by local dogs and children.

At Chinchan we were 14,300 feet high. We had had a light lunch of soup, toast and fruit, but we didn't feel exactly normal. Evidently we had a touch of *soroche,* the mountain sickness. Just then a trainman in a white jacket walked into the car. He was carrying a large rubber bag filled with oxygen. The trainman would hold a nozzle under a passenger's nose and release some oxygen. The passenger would begin to feel better.

We were all glad when we came out of the long tunnel at Galera and started downhill to Huancayo. Although Huancayo is high up (10,696 feet), it is a mile below the high point at Galera tunnel.

We reached the station at 4:10 P.M. and got a generous welcome from Charles Agle of the Peace Corps. He put our luggage into an elderly taxi and took us to the government hotel on the plaza.

Two weeks later we were back in Lima. We wanted to take some pictures of the local train climbing the mountains above the Rimac River. We found an expert driver, Louis Silva, who knew the highway that ran near the railroad. He picked us up in a French Peugeot at 9 o'clock one morning, 90 minutes after the train left. "We shall overtake it," he promised.

Long before we saw the train, we spotted puffs

Nancy Henderson

Passengers at Huancayo. Note the black ribbons on the women's hats.

of black smoke high up and ahead. The train had passed, and the smoke was drifting from tunnels. Since the train had to stop and go backward at some of the switchbacks, we made better time on the highway. Finally we saw the green locomotive and green coaches snaking along the mountainside.

Our driver knew a place where the track ran close by the road. We hurried on, and Nancy Henderson was ready with her camera before the train passed. The fireman waved. Then, for half an hour, we chased the train up the narrow Rimac Valley. First we would get ahead, then wait for the train at a bridge or tunnel. We would hear the awesome blast of the locomotive in the tunnel. Then the train would shoot from the dark hole and cross a bridge high above us.

The trainmen enjoyed this game. Once the fire-man stood on top of the tender and waved. "He wants us to take his picture," our driver explained. Mrs. Henderson obliged.

Gifts from Peru

The famous street market at Huancayo is outside of the Rimac Valley. But Huancayo is the terminal of the Central Railway, which follows the Rimac. And since we have been following the railway, we shall follow it to the market.

Every Sunday the Indians from miles around come to Huancayo. Some travel by truck or bus. Many come on foot. Some bring goods to sell. Others come to buy, or simply to see their friends. There is more to be seen than anyone could see in a day. The sellers expect people to look and seldom try to make a sale. They prefer to sit in silence. Travelers have called the fair "the quietest market in the world."

All traffic is cleared from the main street, a

At the Huancayo market, the main street has three rows of booths.

Nancy Henderson

fairly broad thoroughfare lined with small shops, many of them shabby. Booths are set up along the sidewalks and down the middle of the street. The fair is half a mile long.

The ladies in our party went first to the booths where silver jewelry and alpaca rugs were displayed. Presents were bought for a bride in Detroit and for other friends.

Also admired was a 14-inch water dipper, neatly carved from wood. A llama was shown on the end of the handle and midway was the figure of an Indian playing a harp. This cost 85 cents.

Fruits, vegetables and grain made colorful displays. Neat little piles of each kind were arranged on old blankets, watched over by stolid Indian women wearing the typical white straw hats with black bands. It was not a cold day, but the squatting merchants wore many garments. One had her baby wrapped in a shawl on her back, sound asleep, and a number of small turkeys concealed in her apron, wide awake. Many of these women were large enough to accommodate a variety of merchandise.

Nancy Henderson

Like most of the Indians, these women do not urge anyone to buy.

The medical section of the fair was fascinating. Strange powders, stones, nuts and seeds for treating illness were on sale, spread out in the open air. A dried cat, considered a powerful remedy, was priced at 60 cents. There was a porcupine skin, not in good condition, and a pile of dried

Nancy Henderson

Peruvians carry almost anything on their backs. This is llama wool.

starfish. Certain kinds of beads would improve the health of the wearer, we were told.

A less reputable pharmacist was offering small bottles of a liquid called "Baldo," priced at one *sol* (4 cents). It was recommended for the kidneys and for cancer, and for smoothing out wrinkles.

A list of all the articles for sale would fill two or three books of this size. Here is a small sample:

Mousetraps	Rusty bolts
Sun glasses	Handmade hatchets
Artificial flowers	Brass bells
Hats	Emblems from Ford cars
Guitars and mandolins	Sewing machines
Oil stoves	Old coke bottle tops
Aluminum kettles	Suitcase handles
Dice	Rock salt for animals
Ammunition boxes	Dishes from Hong Kong
Pottery cows and dogs for savings banks	Secondhand comic books (for rent)
Secondhand truck springs	Coat hangers
Horseshoes	Automatic sprinklers
Ball bearings	Beds

Several Indians were gathered around a large carton at the curb. I leaned over to find out what was for sale. The box held hundreds of pieces of movie film, cut to strips of 10 frames each. You could choose any three strips for 2 cents, so I did, without recognizing what I had taken. Later I studied the films with a magnifying glass. One showed a religious parade. Another showed two men in an office. The third strip was in color. A beautiful red-haired woman in a yellow sweater was saying to a gangster-type fellow: "Your partner got away with all the money."

Saddles and leather goods were at one booth. I noticed an old saddle blanket, woven from llama wool. It was bordered with a crisscross pattern in dark brown, and in the center was the silhouette of a brown pitcher. On the side of the pitcher was a flower in bright cerise. Thinking of our cat, I said to my wife that it would be a nice present for Rover. "It's filthy," she said, and indeed it was—the overall shade could have been called either light brown or dark yellow. I asked the price, and was quoted $4. All of my companions warned against what they feared I would do. "No Indian would pay more than $1," one of them said. "But I am not an Indian," I replied.

When we got back to Pennsylvania, I took the heavy blanket to the laundry tub. After five washings the water turned only light brown. Two rinsings followed, and for several days the blanket dripped dry. The background became a clear ivory, and the wool—once stiff and greasy—was soft to the fingers. We spread the blanket before the

Nancy Henderson

A young mother with her child and his dog at the fair.

fireplace one evening. The cat smelled the edges, bobbing his head as cats do when they seek information with their noses about the things that are important to them. Satisfied, he accepted the gift from Peru and curled up before the fire.

65

Tunnel
Through the Andes

The Rimac is one of the hardest working rivers in South America. It begins in a carefree fashion, without any interference from man. High in the Andes, streams from a score of small lakes and ponds come together and form the Rimac. The young river tumbles through its canyon to Surco, a town about 50 miles east of Lima.

At Surco the Rimac goes to work. Its water is diverted to the Callahuanca power station in the Santa Eulalia Valley. This station makes electricity for Lima. The same water is used again at the Moyopampa power station, 2,000 feet lower in

Lima Light and Power Company

Drilling the tunnel to bring water through the Andes to the Rimac.

altitude. This station is at Chosica, just below the junction with the Santa Eulalia River. Next the Rimac spins the turbines at a third power plant farther downstream. This is the Huampani station, across the valley from the town of Chaclacayo.

After being used three times to produce electricity, the Rimac irrigates thousands of desert acres. It provides water for the households and factories of Lima and Callao. Finally it tries to cleanse its bed of a vast amount of trash and sewage contributed by citizens along the way.

With the help of the Santa Eulalia, its main tributary, the Rimac has performed well. But

there is one serious fault in both rivers. They
don't have enough water. For about eight months
in each year they are more like brooks than
rivers.

Lima needs more electricity and more water
every year. The population of the Lima-Callao
area has passed 2,000,000. New industries are
being established and all require water. The engineers of Lima Light and Power Company knew,
years ago, that the Rimac could not meet the
future need. They also knew that the only source

An aqueduct carries Atlantic watershed runoff to the Pacific side.

Nancy Henderson

of more water was the eastern slope of the Andes.

More than two miles above sea level on the Atlantic slope are several sizable lakes, filled by plentiful rains from the eastern trade winds. The lakes drain into the Santa Ana River, which flows into the Mantaro River. The Mantaro empties into the Apurimac, which runs to the Ucayali. And the Ucayali joins the Marañon to form the broad Amazon.

The engineers saw no reason why the water that Lima needed should be emptied, unused, into the Atlantic Ocean. They decided to bring it through the Andes to the Pacific slope. To do this, dams were built on the Atlantic side so water could be stored in the rainy season. An aqueduct was built from the lakes to the mountain that divides the two watersheds.

The biggest job was tunneling six miles through the Andes. Excavating began on the Pacific slope in 1957 and at the Atlantic entrance in 1958. Above the workmen the mountain was one-sixth to one-half mile high. It turned out to be a very wet mountain. Again and again the drillers struck water pockets that flooded the tunnel. One emptied more than 800 gallons a second, and the workers had to run for their lives. Usually the water ran 18 inches deep on the floor of the tunnel. It was close to freezing, with a temperature of 40 degrees Fahrenheit.

Men can't work well in icy water up to their knees. It was hard to haul out rock on the flooded tracks of the narrow gauge railway. The engineers decided to make the tunnel a yard deeper so the water could drain out. Ties for the railway were laid across the drainage ditch and a footbridge was spiked down for the drillers. Thus the men could work above the water instead of in it.

It took almost five years to bore the six-mile tunnel. In 1962 came the breakthrough, when the crews from each end met near the middle.

The tunnel led to the Canchis River on the Pacific slope, where a small reservoir was built. From the reservoir another tunnel was dug for 8½ miles to carry water to a new power station, called Huinco. The tunnel ended high on a

Water plunges down the pipe and spins the turbines of Huinco power station. On this mountainside Señor Mesa pointed to a wreck.

Lima Light and Power Company

mountainside, almost a mile above the Santa Eulalia River.

The engineers wanted the water to plunge downward with maximum force to spin the Huinco turbines. They designed a shaft about 8 feet in diameter and made it almost vertical. The power station had to be built at the foot of the shaft, and the foot of the shaft was inside a mountain. Here the machinery would be safe from huge rocks that sometimes roll down into the valley.

A great hall was blasted out—an underground room—350 feet long, 100 feet wide and 78 feet high. A tunnel big enough for large trucks led to the hall. Turbines, dynamos, cables and all kinds of machinery were hauled through the tunnel.

The water from the other side of the Andes and the great Huinco power plant more than doubled the supply of electricity for Lima. Like the water of the Rimac, the Transandean water is used again and again. The Santa Eulalia River carries it down to Callahuanca and then to the power stations along the Rimac. Finally it goes into Lima's water system.

Lima Light and Power Company

The arrow marks entrance to the underground station at Huinco.

The Transandean project and the Huinco station cost about $62 million. Half of the money was borrowed from the World Bank. Equipment came from Switzerland, Italy, Austria, Peru, Argentina, Japan and the United States.

When the project was planned, there were no roads within miles. There was hardly a level acre. The Andes country has towering peaks and deep, narrow valleys. The first supplies for the surveyors and engineers were hauled on the backs of llamas, following rough trails. Then Lima Light and

73

Nancy Henderson

Señor Mesa at the Atlantic end of the Transandean water tunnel.

Power Company spent several million dollars to build dirt roads wide enough for a truck. We were driven over these roads by Señor Julian Mesa, "one of our very best drivers," said Miss Vera Neuwald of the power company.

Señor Mesa handled his station wagon as a violinist handles his bow. Most of the road was not wide enough for passing. At every sharp curve— and there were hundreds of them—our driver tapped out a rapid five-note warning on his horn. Once we stopped just three feet short of a truck coming around a turn. The truck driver hadn't bothered to sound his horn.

There were no guard rails. Along the precipices stones had been set up every few feet as a reminder of the depths below. We zigzagged down a series of hairpin turns to the Huinco power station and stopped at one point to take pictures. Señor Mesa pointed to something red on the mountainside we had descended. It was the wreck of an automobile. I asked whether the driver had been killed. Señor Mesa laughed at the question. "They are always killed," he said.

The dead are remembered. From time to time we passed crosses at the edge of the road. They were usually made of plain wood, but some had been fashioned from pipe and a few from ornamental iron.

Nancy Henderson

At this point on a road in the Andes, a driver went over the edge.

Lima Today

Lima was once called "the fairest gem on the shores of the Pacific." Those were the words of William H. Prescott, the historian, written more than a century ago. The old Spanish city has changed in many ways, and not always for the better. It has skyscrapers, trolley cars and more electric signs than anyone would care to read. It has the most dilapidated taxicabs in the world. Many of them are 30 years old and lack such items as fenders, hoods and springs.

The streetcars aren't young, either. They are painted a dull gray, toned brown by the city's dust. Many of them carry large signs advertising a popular soft drink, Inka Kola. This stuff is not the conventional brown. It comes in green and yellow.

Lima looks as gray as the winter sky. But at certain times and places it bursts into color. When the president receives a new ambassador from a foreign country, a fairy tale is acted out. The gates of the Government Palace on the Plaza de Armas are opened. Out comes an old-fashioned coach, drawn by two well-brushed horses. The driver wears white gaiters, red pantaloons, a dark blue jacket and a top hat. A troop of cavalry escorts the coach. The soldiers sport red trousers, white tunics and silver helmets.

Bugles blowing, the cavalrymen conduct the coach to the Hotel Bolivar at the Plaza San Martín. The ambassador steps out from the hotel and into the coach for the short ride to the palace. After presenting his credentials, he is driven back to the hotel.

The palace was built in 1938 on the site of the sixteenth century palace of Francisco Pizarro. Nearby is the more interesting Torre Tagle Palace, erected in 1735. This is Lima's finest example of

Nancy Henderson

Trolley cars and taxicabs in Lima were not manufactured yesterday.

Nancy Henderson

Nancy Henderson

The Government Palace guards carry guns that are quite modern.

colonial architecture. It is occupied by the Peruvian Foreign Office, but visitors are permitted in the courtyard. They may also inspect a Moorish balcony, built of carved wood and completely enclosed. Persons on the balcony can look through the shutters without being seen by people on the

80

Nancy Henderson
A Moorish balcony of carved wood on the palace of the archbishop.

streets. A number of these balconies may be seen on other old buildings.

A particularly interesting bridge is the Puente de Piedra, or Stone Bridge, directly behind the Government Palace. It was built in 1610, in the Roman style. To make a strong mortar, the sand

81

and cement were mixed with hundreds of thousands of egg whites. This bridge leads to Cerro San Cristobal, a high hill with a cross visible for miles around.

Lima's tallest building is the headquarters of the Ministry of Education, 22 stories high. And the oldest university of the Americas is San Marcos University, founded in 1551 at the Dominican Monastery. Twenty years later it was separated from the church and moved to other quarters. The new campus lies between Lima and Callao.

Lima has a rich assortment of museums. If you would like to see one of the cannons brought from Spain by Pizarro, go to the Museum of Military History at Callao. If you would like to see Pizarro, you will find him under glass in the cathedral on the Plaza de Armas.

Nancy Henderson

This hut beneath a palm tree is made of woven mats, mud-plastered.

The Squatters

When the Incas ruled Peru, every family had enough land to grow food. The Spaniards took away the land, and the Indians have got back very little. A wealthy 2% of the population owns three-fourths of all the good land.

Many of the landless Indians work on the big

haciendas. The owners provide miserable shanties and miserable food. They also pay cash wages. The pay is as low as 25 centavos, slightly less than one United States cent for a full day's work.

Although Peru's population is growing steadily, its farms have been producing less. Most of the peasants live on the brink of starvation. Hoping to find more to eat, tens of thousands have been coming out of the mountains and down the river valleys to Lima. They have settled along the Rimac and on the hills east of the city. They haven't bought land or rented it. They have simply taken it. Then they have built little shacks, often using woven mats for walls. The shacks stand close together, forming small cities.

The sprawling slums built by the squatters are called *barriadas*, which means "poor neighborhoods." The upper classes of Lima never go into the barriadas. "There are bad people there—they will throw stones at you," one man warned us. There would be plenty to throw, for the ground near the Rimac is covered with water-worn stones.

But we found the people warm and friendly, as

Nancy Henderson

In the barriadas you can get a haircut in the middle of the street.

poor people generally are. We spent two hours walking around, talking, making photographs. Tourists are always quickly spotted by beggars— even the children plead for "Money, money, money!" Not one person in the barriadas asked for money.

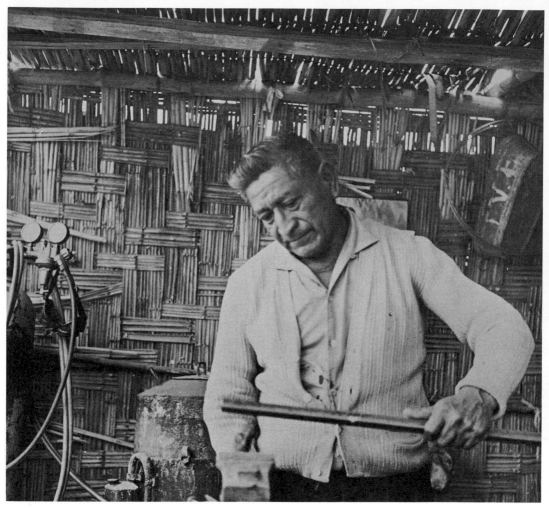

Nancy Henderson

Señor Vasquez does iron work in his house, close by the Rimac.

One man we talked to was Manuel Vasquez, an iron worker, who had lost his house in April 1964. It was washed away by the flooding Rimac. He had built another, close by the river. When he could get work, he earned $1.20 to $1.60 a day.

He had a 20-year-old son and a 16-year-old daughter. The son was a mechanic's helper.

We asked what the family ate on a typical day. For breakfast, it was tea and bread. For lunch, rice and soup. Sometimes the soup had beans, potatoes or tomatoes. The dinner was coffee and bread. Once a week the family bought soup meat for 38 cents a pound. Occasionally they had margarine, but milk and cheese were too expensive.

The streets and vacant land in the barriadas are dirty. Countless dogs sniff among the garbage, hunting for scraps. Because there was no water supply, the government laid pipes and installed faucets here and there. People bring two pails at a time, carrying them at each end of a pole that rests on the shoulder. Like most water in Peru, the water in the barriadas is not pure. It comes from the Rimac, where sewage is dumped. Thousands of Peruvians die each year from water-borne diseases.

The government is building housing projects for workers, but it has not been able to keep up with the growing need. Only 1 person out of every 9

Nancy Henderson

A shoe repair shop (above) and a grocery and soft drink store.

Nancy Henderson

in Peru has a decent house. The population grows faster than the housing supply.

In the mountains, some of the starving Indians have chosen to fight for land. Arming themselves with slingshots and rusty guns, they have marched on many of the big haciendas. Their banners have borne the slogan "Land or Death!" For a little while they occupied lands of the terrified owners. Then the government sent troops and police to evict the peasants. The crude weapons of the Indians were almost useless when the troops opened fire. Many settlers were killed, and the rest were driven away.

But the cry for land has not been silenced. The government has said the big estates must be broken up, and it asks the Indians to be patient. The Indians reply that after waiting more than 400 years, their patience is running out.

End of the River

The Rimac pours into the Pacific at a lonely spot seldom seen by tourists. The closely guarded Naval Arsenal is at the mouth of the river, on the south bank. An officer gave us permission to walk to the beach and sent a sailor with us. We crossed a narrow bridge to the north bank, which was thickly covered with brush and small trees. Cows were grazing in the few grassy openings. One of the cowpaths led to the beach, a vast pile of rounded stones.

The Rimac was swirling through a gap in the stone barrier. The water looked dirty, and it was.

The harbor of Callao is less than a mile south of the Rimac. Scores of fishing boats were tied

Nancy Henderson

The Rimac empties into the Pacific through this narrow channel.

up when we arrived, and pelicans were all over the place. A line of the big brown birds decorated the roof of the pier shed. The alcatraz, as it is called, is the largest member of the pelican family. A fisherman gave us some scraps, which we tossed onto the deck of an abandoned boat. Pelicans swooped down from all directions, landing awkwardly, but quickly scooping up the pieces of fish.

Several fishermen were mending their nets. Each had taken off the shoe from one foot so the net could be held taut with his big toe.

91

Thousands of tons of anchovies are brought into Callao, and most of the catch is shipped out as fishmeal for use in animal feed. Fishmeal has become Peru's most valuable commodity for export. Copper, long the leader, is now in second place. Only Japan tops Peru in fishing.

During the sixteenth century the British buccaneer, Sir Francis Drake, raided the Spanish treasure ships at Callao. In 1746 the town was wiped out by a tidal wave following an earthquake that destroyed Lima. After rebuilding, Callao played an important part in Peru's history. It was here that the Argentine patriot, General José de San Martín, landed in 1820 with his army to win Peru's independence from Spain. The last place in South America to fly the Spanish flag was the fortress of Real Felipe at Callao. A royalist garrison was besieged there for more than a year. The starving survivors finally gave up.

In the war with Chile (1879–1883), Callao was blockaded by an enemy squadron. The Chileans captured one day what they considered a real prize: a drifting boat, crewless, loaded with fresh

Nancy Henderson

Fishermen at Callao hold nets taut with their toes, for mending.

vegetables. Sailors from the man-of-war *Loa*, sick of beans and pork, got the boat alongside and unloaded it. The last item was a bag of potatoes. When it was lifted, the boat blew up and sank the warship. The Chileans had been booby-trapped. The vegetable boat had a hidden torpedo, triggered to explode when the potatoes were removed.

South America's first railroad linked Callao with

Nancy Henderson

Eleven pelicans watch the photographer with a single thought: Fish!

Lima in 1851. Diesel engines now haul carloads of copper, zinc and lead to the docks. Products of the smelter at La Oroya, they are brought over the Andes and down the Rimac Valley on the Central Railway. The. llamas along the highway pay little attention to the whistle of the locomotive. These ancient inhabitants are not disturbed by competition in burden-bearing.

Index

Agle, Charles, 55
Alcatraz, 28
Amazon River, 6, 47, 69
Anchovies, 27, 34, 92
Andes, 3, 5, 7, 8, 14, 16, 35, 36, 41, 44, 48, 66, 69, 72, 73
Arequipa, 40
Atahualpa, 18, 20
Atlantic Ocean, 6, 69

Balconies, 80, 81
Barriadas, 84–88
Boobies, 28, 29, 34

Cajamarca, 18, 21
California, 39–41, 43
Callao, 6, 22, 23, 34, 40, 41, 67, 82, 90, 92, 93
Carbon-14, 13
Cat God, 15
Central Railway, 35, 45, 47, 48, 58, 94
Cerro de Pasco, 45
Cerro de Pasco Copper Corporation, 46
Chapman, Frank M., 28
Chavin culture, 14
Chicla, 44
Chile, 5, 40, 41, 43, 44, 92, 93
Chosica, 12, 50, 51, 67
Churches, 21
Coolies, Chinese, 32, 43
Copper, 22, 45, 46, 94
Cormorants, 28, 31, 34
Corn, 16, 53
Cuzco, 11, 15, 20

Desamparados station, 48
Diamonds, 24
Drake, Sir Francis, 92

Electric power, 66–68, 70, 72, 77
Eucalyptus, 46, 47

Fishing industry, 34, 91
Fishmeal, 34, 92
Frick, Henry Clay, 46

Galera, 41, 55
Garua, 9
Gold, 17, 19–21, 24, 39, 45
Government Palace, 78, 80, 81
Guanayes, 27, 28, 31, 33, 34
Guano, 30–34, 44
Guano Company, 33, 34

Henderson, Nancy, 48, 57
Highways, 7, 12, 13, 47, 55, 57, 74–76, 94
Housing, 84, 86–88
Huancayo, 46–48, 55, 56, 58
Huinco power station, 70–73, 75
Humboldt current, 8, 9, 27

Incas
    Agriculture, 16, 30
    Conquest by Spaniards, 18, 20, 83
    Government, 10, 15
    History, 13, 15
    Honesty, 17
    Language, 13
    Roads, 16, 35
    Stone work, 16, 17
    Wealth, 17, 21
Indians
    Agriculture, 10, 50, 52, 53
    Market day, 58, 60–64
    Occupations, 11, 12, 47
    Population, 11
    Poverty, 83–87, 89
    Rebellions, 26, 89
    Treatment by Spaniards, 25, 26

La Oroya, 36, 40, 41, 44–47, 94
Lima
    Description, 6, 9, 34, 48, 50, 77–82

95

History, 21–25, 43, 92, 94
Use of Rimac, 66, 67, 72
Lima Light & Power Company,
 68, 73, 74
Llamas, 7, 12, 35–37, 39, 45, 73, 94

Mantaro River, 47, 69
Market, 58, 60–64
Medical remedies, 61, 62
Meiggs, Henry, 39–41, 43, 44, 47
Mesa, Julian, 74, 75
Mining, 11, 44–47, 94
Mollendo, 40
Morgan, J. Pierpont, 46
Mount Meiggs, 41, 42
Mules, 41, 45
Murphy, Robert Cushman, 31
Museums, 82

Negroes, 25
Neuwald, Vera, 74

Oroya fever, 41, 42

Pacific Ocean, 5, 6, 27, 90
Paracas culture, 14
Pelicans, 28, 34, 91
Peru
 Description, 5, 6, 8–10, 49, 84
 History, 13, 14, 18, 22, 25, 26,
  32, 33, 38, 44, 92
Piquero, 28, 29
Pizarro, Francisco, 18, 20, 21, 78,
 82
Potatoes, 16
Prescott, William H., 77
Puente de Piedra, 81, 82

Quechua, 7, 13
Quipus, 13

Railroads
 Construction, 36, 38, 40, 41, 43–
  45, 47, 93
 Freight, 35, 45, 47, 94
 Routes, 7, 40, 41, 45, 47, 93
 Travel, 48–50, 53–55, 57
Rainfall, 8, 9, 13, 30
Rimac River
 Description, 6, 9, 50, 68, 84, 90
 Geography, 50–52, 66
 History, 16, 21, 23
 Maps, 4, 23
 Name, 7, 8, 23
 Pollution, 67, 87, 90
 Travel route, 7, 36, 40, 55, 94
 Use for power, 66, 68, 72
Road construction, 73–75

San Bartolomé, 51, 53
San Marcos University, 82
San Martín, José de, 26, 92
Santa Eulalia River, 66, 67, 72
Silva, Luis, 55, 57
Silver, 17, 20–22, 24, 45, 60
Soroche, 36, 55
Spaniards
 Conquest of Peru, 18
 Cruelty to Indians, 18, 26
 History, 13, 18, 21, 92
 Wealth, 21, 24
Sun God, 15
Switchbacks, 38–41, 53, 54, 57

Taxicabs, 77, 79
Torre Tagle Palace, 78
Transandean tunnel, 69–73
Trolley cars, 77, 79

Vasquez, Manuel, 86, 87
Viceroy, 25, 26
von Hagen, Victor W., 16

Wool, 12, 36, 64

ALEXANDER L. CROSBY went to Peru in 1964 to see Machu Picchu, the secret stronghold of the Incas that was rediscovered in 1911. He took a side trip to Huancayo on the Central Railway and was so excited about the Rimac Valley and the railroad that he decided to write a book.

Mr. Crosby is a former newspaperman who has been a free-lance writer since 1944. He wrote *The Colorado* and *The Rio Grande* for this series. He and his wife, Nancy Larrick, live near Quakertown, Pa.

NANCY HENDERSON was born in Hollywood and went to Stanford University, where she majored in political science and was elected to Phi Beta Kappa. Interested in photography since high school, she became a professional in 1949. Her candid shots have appeared in newspapers and magazines, and a series on Peru was selected by the *Encyclopedia Britannica*. Married to Laurance G. Henderson of Washington, D.C., Mrs. Henderson has been active in Capitol Hill politics as a writer and researcher.

The Hendersons and their two children have a house in Georgetown with a swimming pool used intensively by Ginger, a collie, who has her own raft. Chris Henderson accompanied his mother to Peru and photographed his favorite subjects, especially alpacas.

Doris Bowers   *Ann Zane Shanks*

Nancy Henderson